My Spiritual Journey

ISBN 978-1-64178-095-7

We are always looking for talented authors and artists. To submit an idea, please send a brief inquiry to acquisitions@foxchapelpublishing.com.

Printed in Malaysia
First printing

My SPIRITUAL Journey

Written and Illustrated by
JOANNE FINK

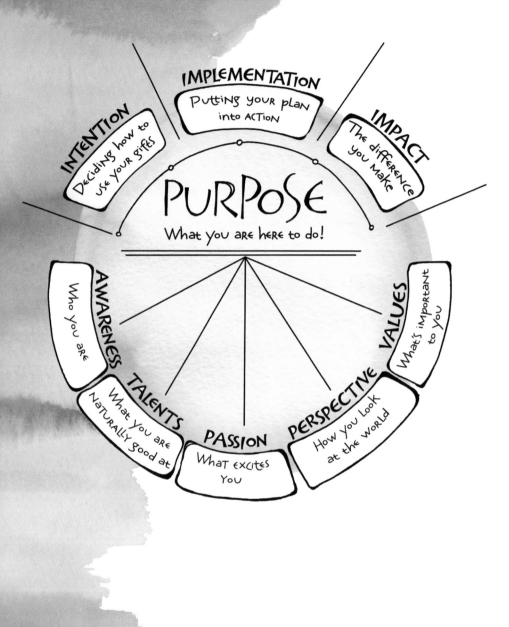

TABLE OF CONTENTS

Discovery

Action

The Ongoing Search
for Insight, Inspiration,
Comprehension & Connection

THE SEARCH FOR MEANING

Who am I?

Where am I headed?

What do I need to grow?

How can I become who I am supposed to be?

INTRODUCTION

This guided journal began with a question—hurriedly written in my morning journal—which led to another question, then another and another.

As the weeks went by, my pen continued to dance over my journal pages, and I realized that the questions I was asking, though thought-provoking, were not necessarily answerable.

But the very act of asking these soul-searching questions was deepening my understanding of who I am and what's important to me. As a spiritual seeker, I am on a continual journey toward the **LIGHT** (my acronym for **L**ove, **I**nspire, **G**ive, **H**eal, **T**ransform). I believe we are all here for a purpose: to use our unique gifts to make a difference in the world.

When you set the intention to be a light in the world—to reach out in **love**, **inspire** by example, **give** from the heart, and help **heal** our broken world— you **transform** yourself in the process. That's soul growth!

To put it in action terms, let the LOVE in your heart INSPIRE you to GIVE of yourself to HEAL and TRANSFORM the world.

If we can remain open to the pain, hope, and joy that are all essential parts of our spiritual journey, everything we experience will help shape us and enable us to grow into the best possible people we are capable of becoming. There are lessons to be learned from each experience if we ask the right questions.

My hope is that this book will help you get to know yourself better; discover your talents, passions, personal perspective, and values; and use what you've learned to determine— and fulfill—your purpose.

LET THE LOVE
IN YOUR HEART
INSPIRE YOU
TO GIVE OF YOURSELF to
HEAL & Transform
THE WORLD

Discovery

The first half of the journal, DISCOVERY, is divided into five subsections: Awareness, Talent, Passion, Perspective, and Values.

Action

The second half, ACTION, has four subsections: Purpose, Intention, Implementation, and Impact.

Each section contains thought-provoking questions and a series of exercises designed to help you write from the heart, discover your core truths, determine your purpose, set intentions, and learn how to share your unique gifts to impact the world in a positive way. There are pages for your questions and reflections as well as places to doodle throughout the journal.

Take your time. The questions and exercises will require some soul searching to complete. This journal, like your life's journey, is meant to be savored, not rushed.

Make this journal your own by coloring some of the illustrations, adding patterns, or writing in different color pens to highlight something that's important. I am excited for you as you embark on this spiritual quest, and I hope you will share parts of your journey by joining and posting in the Zenspirations® Create, Color, Pattern, Play Facebook group.

Remember—you already have all the answers you need inside you.

Blessings on your journey,
Joanne Fink
June 2019

Discovery
Understanding who you are and what's important to you

TALENT
what You are
Naturally
good at

PASSION
what excites you

AWARENESS
who you are

Embarking on this journey of self-discovery and spiritual growth has the power to help you understand yourself and what you feel called to do. You can use that understanding to live a life you love.

As spiritual seekers, we strive for connection with something greater than ourselves. We are blessed when those who accompany us on our journey are kindred spirits who encourage us to shine our inner light and help us connect with our essential selves.

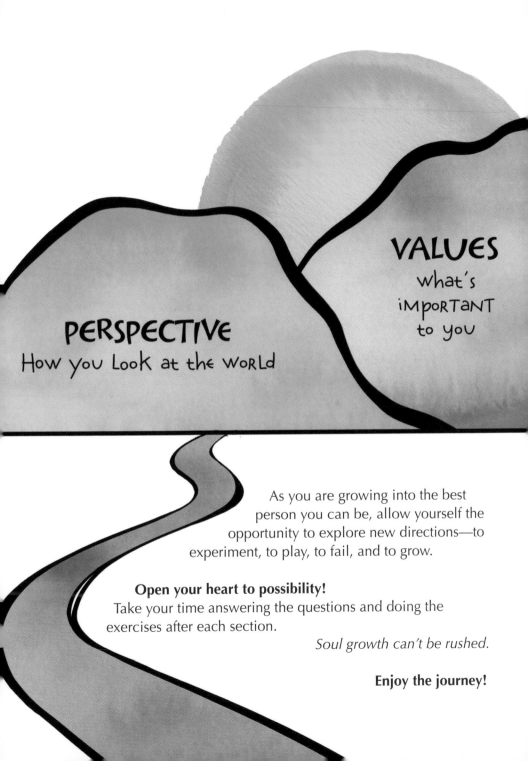

VALUES
what's
iMPORTANT
to you

PERSPECTIVE
How you Look at the WORLD

As you are growing into the best person you can be, allow yourself the opportunity to explore new directions—to experiment, to play, to fail, and to grow.

Open your heart to possibility!
Take your time answering the questions and doing the exercises after each section.

Soul growth can't be rushed.

Enjoy the journey!

Discovery

Who are you at your very core?

DISCOVERY

The diagram below corresponds to the five chapters in the Discovery section: Awareness, Talent, Passion, Perspective, and Values. Who you are at your core is the center of the circle; notice how everything radiates out from there. Discovering what you love, what you are good at, what you believe, how you see the world, and how you can contribute will ultimately help you determine your personal purpose.

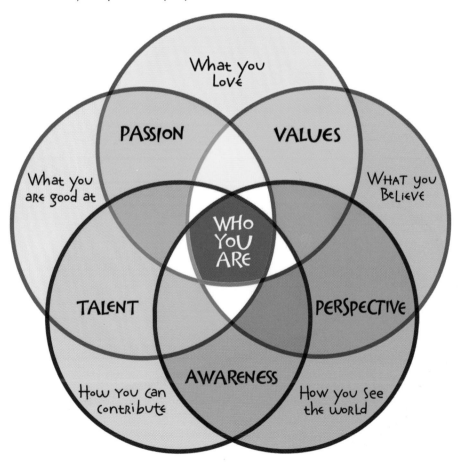

MAKE YOUR LIFE AN INSPIRED JOURNEY

Awareness is an essential part of discovering your spiritual core—what makes you uniquely you.

Living a life that matters begins with a growing awareness of who you are, what you believe, and how you wish to impact the world.

Awareness requires slowing down enough to pay attention to small things. Practice noticing, for example, your instinctive response to situations, the level of tension in your muscles, and what makes you smile.

Cultivate gratitude. Seek connection. Breathe. Be mindful. Be present. Be still. Most importantly, be yourself.

Awareness

WHAT DO YOU hope to LEARN ABOUT YOURSELF?

What makes you unique?

_____
_____
_____
_____
_____
_____
_____
_____

What are your inner strengths?

_____
_____
_____
_____
_____
_____
_____

What do you Like about yourself?

_____

_____

_____

_____

_____

_____

What would you Like to change about yourself?

_____

_____

_____

_____

_____

_____

_____

_____

_____

_____

What DO YOU LOVE most
ABOUT YOUR FAMILY?

_____
_____
_____
_____
_____
_____
_____

What DO you LOVE most
ABOUT YOUR COMMUNITY?

_____
_____
_____
_____
_____
_____
_____

What do you love
most about your life?

Where do you feel
most at home?

_____
_____
_____
_____
_____
_____
_____
_____
_____

FOLLOW THE PATH
YOUR HEART HAS
EMBRACED
AND YOU'LL ARRIVE
AT THE PLACE
YOUR **SOUL**
CALLS HOME

What Do
you want people to
KNow about you?

Doodle or JOuRNaL YOUR aNSWeRS!

What qualities do
you most admire in others?

What qualities do
you strive to embody?

What or who do you
look to for guidance?

ON OUR JOURNEY, WE ARE CALLED UPON TO PLAY DIFFERENT ROLES— SUCH AS FRIEND, TEACHER, VOLUNTEER, STUDENT, MENTOR, EMPLOYEE...

_____

_____

_____

_____

_____

What ROLES have you played in the past?

What ROLES ARE you playing Now?

_____

_____

_____

_____

_____

_____

_____

_____

_____

_____

_____

_____

_____

How are these roles connected?

SURROUND
YOURSELF
WITH PEOPLE
WHO ALLOW
YOU TO
SHINE

If you could
spend time with
anyone, who
would it be?

What are You proud of?

What brings you joy?

what do you regret?

_____
_____
_____
_____
_____
_____
_____
_____
_____
_____
_____
_____
_____
_____
_____
_____
_____
_____
_____
_____
_____
_____
_____

Can you tell what makes you anxious?

_____

_____

_____

_____

_____

How do you handle your anxiety?

_____

_____

_____

_____

How do you handle stress?

How do you silence the
negative voices in your head?

We tend to oNLY share certain parts of our essential selves. Who are You at Your CoRe?

What would people see if you removed the mask you usually wear?

What are You willing To Let go of iN order to grow?

_____

_____

_____

_____   HOW DO

_____   YOU LET

_____   GO OF

_____   ALL THE

_____   THINGS

_____   THAT

_____   PREVENT

_____   YOU FROM

_____   TAKING

_____   *flight*

_____

_____

_____

When
WAS THE LAST TIME
YOU STEPPED OUTSIDE
YOUR COMFORT ZONE?

_____

_____

_____

_____

_____

_____

How do you express yourself creatively?

Doodle or
journal your answers!

WHAT DOES
YOUR SOUL NEED TO SOAR?

Spiritual Seeking

The Art
of Discovering

Layer by Layer,
the inherent **CONNECTION**
to our true selves.

What do you CONSIDER Sacred?

What is the PRAYER YOUR heart keeps whispering?

WHAt aRE YOUR PERSONAL pathways to CONNECtioN?

_____
_____
_____
_____
_____
_____
_____
_____
_____
_____
_____
_____
_____
_____
_____
_____
_____
_____
_____
_____

What RITUALS / SPIRITUAL PRACTICES have
you developed to help you find CONNECTION?

_____

_____

_____

_____

What ROLE DOES faith play IN YOUR LIFE?

_____

_____

_____

_____

_____

_____

_____

_____

_____

_____

STRIVE
Not foR
PeRFECtioN,
but foR
Connection

HOW DOES
CONNECTING WITH
a POWER GREATER
THAN YOURSELF
TRANSFORM
YOU?

POWER of CONNECTION

C·O·N·N·E·C·T·I·O·N
to our true selves
enhances and deepens
our connection with
all living things.

Who HAS BeeN the biggest influence, PositiVE oR NegatiVE, on How You LiVE your Life?

_____

_____

_____

_____

_____

_____

_____

_____

_____

_____

How Do other PeopLe's opiNioNs iNfluence YouR ActioNs?

Who's YouR tribe?

AWARENESS EXERCISE: DISCOVERING YOUR BEST QUALITIES.

Make a list of what you believe to be your best qualities.

Without divulging your list, ask three people you feel close to what they think your best qualities are.

_____ thinks my best qualities are:

_____ thinks my best qualities are:

_____ thinks my best qualities are:

What did people say that you found surprising?

_____

_____

_____

_____

Use the circles to record any commonalities among the answers. Be sure to include your answers.

Open Your Heart to Possibility

When we hear the word *talent*, we tend to think it refers to creative pastimes such as music, art, drama, and writing.

We are all blessed with multiple gifts—natural abilities that are ours to use and share.

You may be a great organizer, super at math, and have a green thumb. You may know someone who is a good listener, a wonderful teacher, or has an innate understanding of technology.

If we remain open to possibility, we often discover that we excel at something we never imagined we could do.

Talent

WHaT aRE YoU NATURALLY GooD at?

_____
_____
_____
_____
_____
_____
_____
_____
_____
_____
_____
_____
_____
_____
_____
_____
_____
_____

WHAT HAVE others
tOLD YOU THAT
YOU ARE GOOD At?

UR thoughts!

How are you using your talents to make a difference in the world?

What is something that your unique gifts make it easy for you to do?

Each of us must find our own special song and sing it to the WORLD

What do you think are YOUR STRONGEST abilities?

Which of YOUR TALENTS have YOU put TIME into DEVELOPING?

WHAT SONG DOES YOUR heart LONG to SING?

TALENT EXERCISE: VOLUNTEERING
Using your talents to make a difference in the world.

List your talents. Include both innate abilities—such as being artistic or athletic—and skills you've developed, such as bookkeeping or writing. Then rate each talent on a 1–10 scale, where 1 means it depletes your energy and 10 means it sparks intense energy.

My Talents & Skills Include:	Energy Level:

Now consider organizations, communities, and causes you support or would like to support. Ask yourself which could benefit from someone with your talents and skills. If none come to mind, Charity Watch, Charity Navigator, and your local community's city government office have lists available. Pick at least three organizations, including at least one that you are not currently involved with, and research what kinds of volunteer help and support they may need. Use the chart on the next page to collect information. Match the needs with your top talents, rank them in order of what calls to your soul, and sign up!

Talent	Organization	Volunteer Opportunity	Frequency

I plaN to uSe MY TaLeNTs oN Behalf of:

_____

Once you determine where your talents can make a difference for others, decide how much time you can commit to your volunteer activities. Track how often and how long you volunteer, and how energized it makes you feel.

Date	Task	Hours	Organization	Energy

Live WITH PROMISE
Love WITH PASSION
Laugh WITH PLEASURE

Passion is the energetic excitement and deep sense of satisfaction we get from doing something we love. It drives us to devote ourselves to causes we believe in. Passion makes us lose track of time and motivates us to make things happen.

Passion is the exhilarated feeling we get doing something truly fulfilling.

Your passion might be your work, but you can also be passionate about sharing your special gifts to benefit a cause that's important to you. Whether by creating art, parenting, gardening, being a community leader, running a marathon, knitting hats for newborns, or whatever it is you love to do, we all have the opportunity to make a positive difference in our own little corner of the world by doing what we love.

Passion lights us up and fuels our purpose.

It is possible to have multiple passions and to discover new ones throughout our lives, so make time to explore new things.

Do what you love and you will always love what you do!

Passion

WHAT REALLY excites YOU?

_____
_____
_____
_____
_____
_____
_____
_____
_____
_____
_____
_____
_____
_____
_____
_____
_____
_____
_____

WHAT MAKES YOU LOSE TRACK OF TIME?

JOURNAL or
doodle YOUR
thoughts!

Which of your talents
align with your passions?

What
intrigues
you?

What
Lights You
up?

What causes
are you
passionate
about?
— ♥ —

How can you
contribute
to them?

Allow your
soul to
Dream

Doodle or
journal
your answers

What do you dream about doing?

What dreams are you currently bringing to fruition?

_____
_____
_____
_____
_____
_____
_____
_____
_____
_____
_____
_____
_____

PASSION EXERCISE: FINDING YOUR FLOW (1 MONTH)
Exploring activities that put you in a state of Flow.

Flow is a state of creative focus that allows us to truly concentrate on the task at hand. When you are in a state of flow, you are so totally immersed in the moment that you lose track of time. Some people refer to the flow state as being "in the zone"; it's an altered state of consciousness that takes us outside of ourselves and brings greater clarity, energy, and serenity. It's easiest to enter the flow state when you are doing something that excites and challenges you.

Think about the things you do almost every week, and mentally divide them into three categories: flow, neutral, and chore activities. A FLOW activity makes you lose track of time; a NEUTRAL activity is one you don't mind doing but doesn't excite you, and a CHORE activity is one you would prefer not to do.

Complete for each type of activity: Flow, Neutral, and Chore

Type of Activity	Activity	How I Felt Before	How I Felt During	How I Felt After
FLOW				
NEUTRAL				
CHORE				

For the next month, use the boxes below to record where you were and what you were doing each time you entered a state of Flow.

Most activities that put you in a state of Flow can be considered passions. When we understand our passions—both for what we truly love to do, as well as causes that touch our hearts and inspire us to contribute our talents to make a difference—we are better able to identify our unique purpose. After tracking your Flow states for a month, make a list of your passions below.

My paSsioNs incLude:

_____

_____

_____

_____

_____

_____

You caNNot
ALways change
the WoRld ARouND you,
but you caN change
HoW You Look
At the WoRLD.

Whether something is a BLESSING, a LIFE LESSON, an INJUSTICE, an OBLIGATION, or an OPPORTUNITY depends on how we look at it. Our unique perspective on life begins to form when we are young, and is heavily influenced by our experiences and the people we encounter, as well as how and where we are raised.

Understanding how our personal perspective influences our actions allows us to stand in our truth while remaining open to other viewpoints.

Sometimes the road we travel is bumpy, and it helps to remember that although **we don't get to choose what happens to us, we do get to choose how we react and respond.**

How do you look at the world?

_____

_____

_____

_____

_____

_____

_____

_____

_____

_____

_____

_____

_____

_____

_____

_____

_____

How do you
iNStinctiveLY
REaCt to Change?
Is it FROM a placE
of LovE oR fEaR?

Love
IS
STRONGER
THAN FEAR

EVERYthing
CHANGES...
theN
why
is it
SO
difficuLt
to EMbraCE
CHANGE?

_____

_____

_____

_____

_____

_____

_____

_____

_____

_____

_____

_____

_____

_____

_____

_____

_____

How have the challenges you've faced influenced the path you are on today?

_____
_____
_____
_____
_____
_____
_____
_____
_____
_____
_____
_____
_____
_____
_____

EVERY CHALLENGE, EVERY SETBACK, EVERY DISAPPOINTMENT IS A LEARNING OPPORTUNITY...

How can you stand in your truth while allowing others to stand in theirs?

How have your views on life changed over the past decade?

What UNIQUE perspective on Life did You gain growing up iN YOUR family?

what RECENt expERiENCE OR EVENT has Caused a Shift iN YOUR PERSpective?

Look for the
BLESSING
IN EVERY
SITUATION
especially the
most difficult ones

When you are
dealing with a
serious challenge,
who or what may
be able to help
you look at the
situation through
a different lens?

_____
_____
_____
_____
_____
_____
_____
_____

What unexpected blessing has resulted from something you wish hadn't happened?

_____

_____

_____

_____

_____

_____

_____

_____

_____

Challenges force our souls to grow in new directions

PERSPECTIVE EXERCISE: 5 WAYS TO PRACTICE POSITIVITY

Having a positive perspective or optimistic outlook has been linked to better health and greater happiness, and there are simple exercises we can do to practice positivity. You can do these exercises sequentially or simultaneously.

PRACTICING POSITIVITY BY GROWING IN AWARENESS (24 HOURS)

One of the first steps in practicing positivity is becoming aware of negativity. Listen to the ongoing chatter in your head. Do you talk to yourself as kindly as you would talk to someone you love, or do you constantly criticize yourself? For the next 24 hours, notice negative thoughts (as they arise about situations, others, and, yourself) and without judgment if possible, notice your instinctive reactions and stop yourself before saying or doing anything. When you become aware of a negative thought, use the chart below to write it down, and then write down how you could reframe your thought in a more positive light. For example, if your negative thought is "I am SO stupid!", you could reframe it as "I'm doing my best despite challenging circumstances." Or if you think, "They'll never be able to do this," you could reframe it as "Maybe no one ever taught them how to do this—I will ask if they'd like lessons."

Negative Thought:	Negative Thought Reframed:

PRACTICING POSITIVITY IN OUR SPEECH (24 HOURS)

For the next 24 hours, practice positive self-talk and speech by choosing words that are uplifting, inspiring, and encouraging. Do not say anything negative about anything or anyone, yourself included. After 24 hours, review your positive perspective.

How challenging was practicing positive self-talk?

How did practicing spoken positivity make you feel?

How could you increase positivity the next time you do this exercise?

PRACTICING POSITIVITY BY GROWING IN GRATITUDE (3 WEEKS)

Positive people are aware of and appreciate their blessings! You can grow in gratitude by spending a few minutes each day keeping a gratitude list. Every evening before bed, use the Gratitude Tracker on the next pages to write down three things for which you are grateful. As you go through your day, look for things you can add to your list that night.

GRATITUDE TRACKER

I am grateful FOR THESE three things TODAY.

DATE:
1.
2.
3.

DATE:
1.
2.
3.

DATE:
1.
2.
3.

DATE:
1.
2.
3.

DATE:
1.
2.
3.

DATE:
1.
2.
3.

DATE:
1.
2.
3.

DATE:
1.
2.
3.

DATE:
1.
2.
3.

DATE:
1.
2.
3.

DATE:

1. _____
2. _____
3. _____

DATE:

1. _____
2. _____
3. _____

DATE:

1. _____
2. _____
3. _____

DATE:

1. _____
2. _____
3. _____

DATE:

1. _____
2. _____
3. _____

DATE:

1. _____
2. _____
3. _____

DATE:

1. _____
2. _____
3. _____

DATE:

1. _____
2. _____
3. _____

DATE:

1. _____
2. _____
3. _____

DATE:

1. _____
2. _____
3. _____

DATE:

1. _____
2. _____
3. _____

DATE:

1. _____
2. _____
3. _____

PERSPECTIVE EXERCISE: 5 WAYS TO PRACTICE POSITIVITY *(continued)*

PRACTICING POSITIVITY IN OUR ATTITUDE: (1 MONTH)

Using a scale of 1 to 10, where 1 is a negative attitude and 10 is the most positive you've ever been, record how positive you are over the next month on the Positivity Tracker below. Doodle or write what helps you stay positive in the center circle.

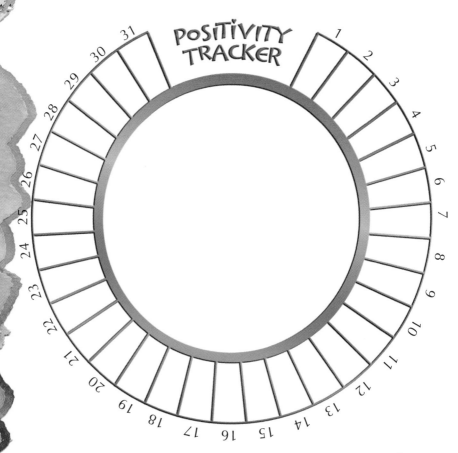

HELPFUL HINT: It's easier to maintain a cheerful disposition when you surround yourself with positive people. Give yourself permission to minimize unnecessary interactions with negative people.

PRACTICING POSITIVITY BY EMULATING POSITIVE PEOPLE: (1 MONTH)

Positivity, like kindness, is contagious! List several of the most positive people you know in the box below.

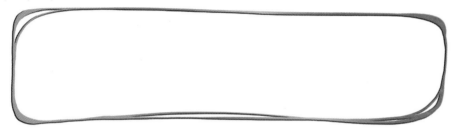

Each week for the next month, try to meet with one of these people (virtual visits are fine if you can't get together in person) and ask how they maintain a positive outlook.

maintaiNS A poSiTiVe ouTLook bY:

MaiNtaiNS a PoSiTiVe outlook By:

MaiNtaiNS a poSiTiVe ouTLook by:

maintains a poSiTiVe ouTLook by:

YOUR CHOICES DEFINE YOU

There are certain things we each value so highly that they are essential to our very being; these are our core values.

Many people value justice, integrity, freedom, and honesty; others value family, faith, fitness, and community. Sometimes one value can encompass several others. Love, for example, can include affection, compassion, caring, generosity, kindness, and trust.

Our values are a reflection of who we are, who we wish to be, and what's most important to us. They are a testament to our character and provide the framework for our purpose. Identifying our values helps us clarify what we stand for and what we ultimately want to be known for.

What's really important to you?

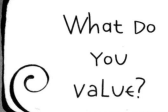

What Do You value?

_____
_____
_____
_____
_____
_____
_____

What Lifelong dream do you wish to fulfill?

_____
_____
_____
_____
_____
_____
_____
_____
_____
_____

What would you do if you could do anything you wanted?

_____
_____
_____
_____
_____
_____
_____

When have you sat in silence
Long enough to become
comfortable with its friendship?

Do you
believe in
your dreams
enough to
devote your life
to making
them happen?

What are
you willing
to fight for?

What Life experiences have had a significant influence on what you value today?

_____

_____

_____

_____

_____

_____

_____

_____

_____

what gives your soul a sense of

SERENITY

VALUES EXERCISE 1: IDENTIFYING YOUR CORE VALUES

Review the list of 100 common core values below, and put checks next to the values that are most important to you. If you have a value that isn't on the list, add it.

❏ Acceptance
❏ Adaptability
❏ Adventure
❏ Advocacy
❏ Appreciation
❏ Approachability
❏ Balance
❏ Belonging
❏ Caring
❏ Charity
❏ Collaboration
❏ Commitment
❏ Community
❏ Compassion
❏ Connection
❏ Consistency
❏ Cooperation
❏ Courage
❏ Creativity
❏ Curiosity
❏ Decisiveness
❏ Dedication
❏ Dependability
❏ Determination
❏ Discipline
❏ Diversity
❏ Education
❏ Efficiency

❏ Empathy
❏ Encouragement
❏ Enthusiasm
❏ Environmentalism
❏ Equality
❏ Excellence
❏ Fairness
❏ Faith
❏ Family
❏ Fitness
❏ Flexibility
❏ Forgiveness
❏ Freedom
❏ Friendships
❏ Fun
❏ Generosity
❏ Giving Back
❏ Gratitude
❏ Growth
❏ Happiness
❏ Harmony
❏ Health
❏ Heritage
❏ Honesty
❏ Humility
❏ Humor
❏ Imagination
❏ Impact

- ❏ Inclusiveness
- ❏ Independence
- ❏ Individuality
- ❏ Innovation
- ❏ Integrity
- ❏ Involvement
- ❏ Joy
- ❏ Justice
- ❏ Kindness
- ❏ Knowledge
- ❏ Leadership
- ❏ Learning
- ❏ Love
- ❏ Loyalty
- ❏ Making a difference
- ❏ Open-mindedness
- ❏ Openness
- ❏ Passion
- ❏ Patriotism
- ❏ Peace
- ❏ Positivity
- ❏ Prayer

- ❏ Preparedness
- ❏ Productivity
- ❏ Professionalism
- ❏ Recognition
- ❏ Reliability
- ❏ Respect
- ❏ Responsibility
- ❏ Security
- ❏ Self-care
- ❏ Selflessness
- ❏ Service
- ❏ Spirituality
- ❏ Stability
- ❏ Stamina
- ❏ Success
- ❏ Thankfulness
- ❏ Thoughtfulness
- ❏ Trustworthiness
- ❏ Uniqueness
- ❏ Wealth
- ❏ Wellbeing
- ❏ Wisdom

❏ _____

❏ _____

❏ _____

❏ _____

❏ _____

❏ _____

❏ _____

❏ _____

VALUES EXERCISE 2: IDENTIFYING YOUR CORE VALUES

Write the values you checked off in the blocks below. Draw additional boxes as needed. Group similar values together by highlighting them in the same color or writing them near each other.

For each group, select one of the values as the core value, and write it at the top of a circle below in bold letters. Add the other values in the group in smaller letters. Use any extra circles to illustrate your core values.

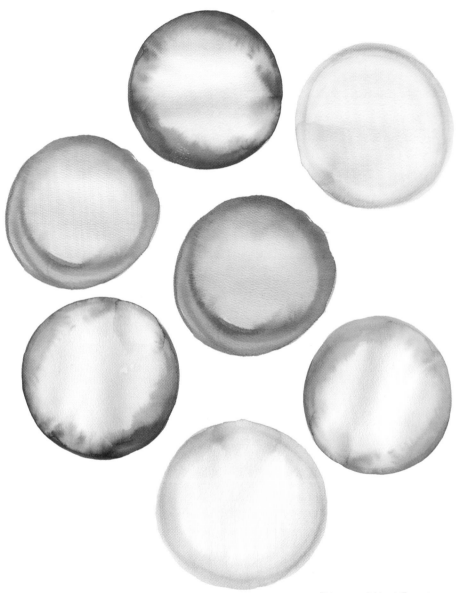

Discovery

What have you DISCOVERED ON YOUR JOURNEY?

Doodle
or JOURNAL
YOUR thoughts.

Action

Using what's important to you to guide your journey of transforming yourself and the world.

PURPOSE
What you are here to do

INTENTION
Deciding how to use your gifts to make a difference

As spiritual seekers, we are on a continual journey toward the LIGHT—to better understand who we are, so we may discover our true calling.

As we continue the process of self-discovery, we gain clarity about our individual purpose for being, and we can explore creative ways of using our natural gifts to make the world a better place.

As you are growing into the best person you can be, look for opportunities to connect with others on similar paths. Share your heart, your abilities, and your mission. And take your time—remember, **soul growth can't be rushed!**

IMPLEMENTATION
Putting your plan into action

IMPACT
The difference you are making

You have a purpose for being on this earth! The exercises in this section are designed to help you discover—and fulfill—this purpose. As before, take your time answering the questions and doing the exercises.

Listen to your heart. Seek connection. Trust that you have what you need to choose the right path. Find and embrace your calling, and take the time you need to thoughtfully implement your intentions. Fulfilling your purpose will require courage, dedication, patience, and love. It is the gift you are giving to yourself; it is the gift you are giving to the world.

Changing the world takes time.

Enjoy the journey!

Action

L♥ve
IS aN
action
VERB
Live a Life You Love!

ACTION

The diagram below corresponds to the four chapters in the Action section: Purpose, Intention, Implementation, and Impact. Why you are here is the center of this circle; what you feel called to do, how you plan to do it, how you are changing the world, and the difference you make radiate out from there. Determining your unique purpose is the first step in living an intentional life, one where you thoughtfully impact your environment and make a difference in the world.

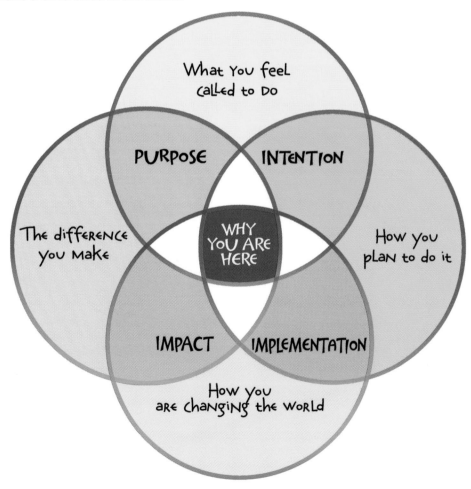

Live BY INSPIRING OTHERS TO FLY

Purpose is the gateway through which we realize our dreams. It gives us a reason to get up in the morning, and helps us live intentional lives. It is possible to have different purposes at different points in our lives, or even several purposes at any one point in time.

While we are all here for a reason—to use our gifts to positively impact the world—our individual purposes can vary greatly. Your purpose might be something close to home: to be a great parent, to be a truly caring friend, or make sure your neighborhood is safe. It could be something you feel called to do based on your life's experience. For example, if you have an autistic child, you may devote yourself to autism awareness; if you lost a loved one to breast cancer, you might raise money to eradicate the disease. Your purpose may be tied to a cause, such as ending hunger, ensuring equal access to education, or saving endangered species.

We each have a purpose for being on this earth that is far more important than anything we have ever dared to imagine. We can change the world—or at least our little corner of it.

Purpose

What is your Mission?

_____

_____

_____

_____

_____

_____

_____

_____

_____

_____

_____

_____

_____

_____

_____

_____

How have the DISCOVERIES you've Made
helped you to UNDERStaND YOUR PURPOSE?

_____

_____

_____

_____

_____

_____

_____

_____

_____

WHat WOULD
YOU DO IF YOU
WeRe TRULY FRee
to Be WHO YOU ARE?

WHAT do
YOU feeL
CALLed to Do?

What RESOURCES
ARE available to
heLp YOU do it?

_____

_____

_____

_____

_____

_____

_____

_____

_____

_____

_____

_____

_____

_____

_____

What fuels
your purpose?

_____
_____
_____
_____
_____
_____
_____
_____
_____
_____
_____
_____

WHAT CALLS
to YOUR SOUL?

_____
_____
_____
_____
_____
_____
_____
_____
_____
_____
_____
_____

Awaken
TO YOUR LIFE'S TRUE
P·U·R·P·O·S·E

WHAT LIFELONG DREAM
do you wish to FULFILL?

_____
_____
_____
_____
_____
_____
_____
_____
_____
_____
_____

What gives
you Hope?

_____
_____
_____
_____
_____
_____
_____
_____
_____

PURPOSE EXERCISE: DETERMINING YOUR PERSONAL PURPOSE

Using what you've learned about yourself, fill in the boxes below.

Based on awareness of who I am, I feel called to:

Based on my innate abilities, I feel called to:

Based on my passions, I feel called to:

Based on my personal perspective, I feel called to:

Based on my core values, I feel called to:

PURPOSE
What you are here to do!

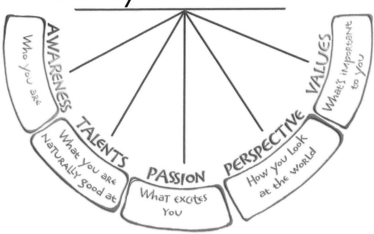

AWARENESS — Who you are

TALENTS — What you are naturally good at

PASSION — What excites you

PERSPECTIVE — How you look at the world

VALUES — What's important to you

Write your personal purpose in the box below.

MY purpose is...

_____

_____

_____

_____

_____

_____

_____

_____

_____

_____

_____

_____

_____

_____

_____

_____

_____

_____

Questions

Reflections

My heart is wondering...

live
WITH
INTENTION

Intention is the starting point of fulfilling our life's purpose. Setting intentions allows us to focus on the specific difference we want to make in the world.

Intentions that genuinely reflect what we feel called to do provide a road map with which we can better navigate our life's journey.

Make your intentions specific and measurable; writing them down makes it easier to put them into action. Review them often, and use them to help realize your dreams as you work toward implementing your purpose.

Let your intentions be a guiding star to shine light on your path.

Intention

As I continue my journey, I intend...

_____
_____
_____
_____
_____
_____
_____
_____
_____
_____
_____
_____
_____
_____
_____
_____

WHAT *really* MATTERS TO YOU?

WHAT ARE YOU DOING TO REALLY
MAKE YOUR LIFE MATTER?

IF Life IS a Gift,

who or what are you giving yours to?

_____

_____

_____

_____

_____

_____

_____

How do your values and purpose guide your intentions?

_____

_____

_____

_____

_____

_____

What intentions have you set that will make today a day worth remembering?

BE A LIGHT INTO THE WORLD

LOVE
INSPIRE
GIVE
HEAL
TRANSFORM

Doodle or Journal your Thoughts

Who will you turn to for support in implementing your intentions?

BE FEARLESS

DO NOT LET FEAR KEEP YOU FROM LIVING A LIFE of MEANING & PURPOSE

How DO YOU live your life so that it HAS meaning?

What DO YOU want YOUR LEGACY to Be?

_____
_____
_____
_____
_____
_____
_____
_____
_____

INTENTION EXERCISE: SETTING YOUR INTENTIONS

Most people are multifaceted, walking in different worlds.
We may be members of various communities such as family,
school, work, book club, religious group, sporting team,
sorority, or pool friends. List the different groups to which
you belong in the spaces below.

Reflect on your purpose(s) while thinking about the different communities to which you belong. Pick the ones that are most closely aligned with your highest purpose(s), and set specific intentions to use your gifts to positively impact these four communities. Complete a Statement of Intention for each.

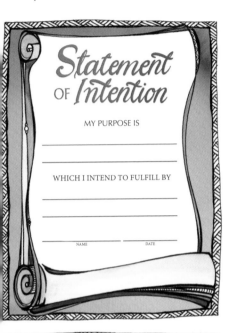

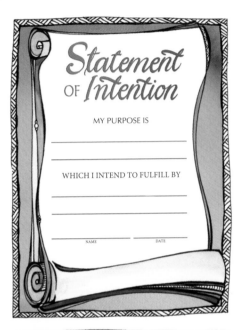

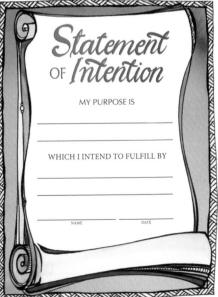

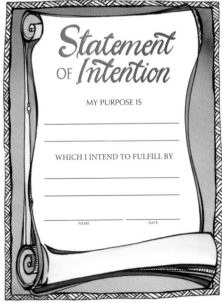

Setting these intentions...

Questions

Reflections

My heart is wondering...

A SINGLE *loving* ACT CAN TRANSFORM THE WORLD

Implementation is the bridge between intention and impact. Implementing our intentions takes them out of the conceptual into the actual. It's how we fulfill our purpose and make things happen. Taking intentional action based on our values allows us to have a meaningful impact on the people, causes, and communities we love.

Dreaming about the change you'd like to see is great, but the reality is that you are the only one who can fulfill your purpose.

When you have the ability to make a difference, you also have a responsibility to act.

There are many ways to achieve your goals—pick one that feels right to you. Begin where you are. Believe in yourself and your dreams. Don't be afraid to ask for help. Implementation requires vision, courage, patience, and determination. If you continually take small, concrete steps toward your goals, you will be amazed at what you can accomplish.

Implementation

What simple changes can you make that will have big benefits a year from now?

_____
_____
_____
_____
_____
_____
_____
_____
_____
_____
_____
_____
_____
_____
_____
_____
_____
_____

WHAT are you doing to implement your intentions?

_____
_____
_____
_____
_____

HOW does this action fuel your purpose?

_____
_____
_____
_____
_____
_____
_____
_____
_____

WHAT stands in the way of implementing your intentions?

_____
_____
_____
_____
_____
_____
_____
_____
_____
_____

HOW do YOU want to CONTRIBUTE?

WHEN AND HOW WILL YOU BEGIN?

Forgiveness

IS A GIFT
YOU GIVE

Yourself

YOU
CANNOT
BE FREE
WHEN
YOU ARE ANGRY

YOU CANNOT MOVE FORWARD WITH YOUR LIFE
WHEN YOU ARE STUCK
IN THE PRISON
OF YOUR PAST

YOU CANNOT TRULY BE WHOLE
WHEN YOU HARBOR RESENTMENT
IN YOUR SOUL

FORGIVENESS IS A GIFT~
GIVE IT TO YOURSELF!

From whom do you seek forgiveness?

_____

_____

_____

_____

Who do you regret hurting? Have you apologized and asked for forgiveness?

_____

_____

_____

_____

Have you been forgiven?
Have you forgiven yourself?

_____

_____

_____

_____

What kind things are you doing FOR YOURSELF?

WHAT KIND THINGS ARE YOU DOING FOR YOUR FRIENDS?

What kind things are you doing for your family?

What kind things are you doing for others?

_____

_____

Neighbors?

_____

_____

Strangers?

_____

_____

Service Workers?

_____

_____

IMPLEMENTATION EXERCISE: MULTIPLE PATHS TO THE SAME GOAL

Most purpose-based intentions can be implemented in a variety of ways. For example, if your purpose is to end breast cancer, you might set an intention to raise money for breast cancer research, or to raise awareness about mammograms. You could implement these intentions by holding a fundraiser, participating in a fundraising walk or run, starting a social media campaign, reminding friends to schedule their annual check-up, or offering to organize a lecture series. All of these implementation strategies help achieve the same goal: eradicating breast cancer.

What implementation strategies have you applied to the intentions you've set? Use the chart below to list three additional strategies.

I set an intention to

_____

Different ways I can implement this intention include:

_____

_____

_____

Ask three people you trust which of your implementation strategies they think have promise. Record their answers in the boxes below.

Small actions today can lead to real impact in your life and the lives of others over time. Fill in the chart below to see how you will shine your light in the world.

I plaN to uSe the folLowiNg iMpleMeNtatioN StraTegie5

_____

_____

_____

HELPFUL HINT: Invite others to join you as you work toward fulfilling your purpose.

These actions will...

_____

_____

_____

_____

_____

_____

_____

_____

_____

_____

_____

_____

_____

_____

_____

_____

_____

Questions

Reflections

My heart is wondering...

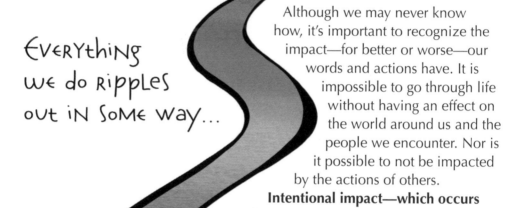

EVERYthiNG
wE do RippLES
ouT iN SoME way...

Although we may never know
how, it's important to recognize the
impact—for better or worse—our
words and actions have. It is
impossible to go through life
without having an effect on
the world around us and the
people we encounter. Nor is
it possible to not be impacted
by the actions of others.
**Intentional impact—which occurs
when our actions are in alignment with
our values and intentions—gives us the
opportunity to fulfill our highest purpose.**

We are where we are thanks to the numerous people
who blazed trails and planted seeds for their progeny.
Let's pay it forward! When you take responsibility for the
way your attitude and actions impact those around
you, the world we live in instantaneously and
imperceptibly shifts for the better.

Impact

Who has had a profound impact on your life?

DISCOVER

YOUR CONNECTION TO THE LIGHT
THAT CONTINUALLY BURNS IN YOUR SOUL.
·IT IS THE LIGHT OF PASSION·
·IT IS THE LIGHT OF CREATIVITY·

IT IS THE
LIGHT OF
LOVE

WHEN YOU LOOK THROUGH THE EYES OF LOVE,
YOU REALIZE EACH PERSON YOU MEET
HAS U·N·L·I·M·I·T·E·D POTENTIAL.
·LOOK WITH LOVE·
AND YOU'LL SEE PROMISE INSTEAD OF LIMITATION,
AND BEAUTY INSTEAD OF IMPERFECTION.
·WHEN LOVE FILLS YOUR HEART·
THERE ISN'T ROOM FOR FEAR AND NEGATIVITY.
·LOOK WITH LOVE·
AND YOU'LL SEE PAST SOMEONE'S CHARACTER FLAWS
TO THE SPARK OF HOLINESS INSIDE THEIR SOUL.

What makes you feel Loved?

_____

_____

_____

_____

_____

_____

How do you express Love?

_____

_____

_____

_____

_____

_____

How are you using Love as a force for good?

_____

_____

_____

_____

_____

_____

IMPACT EXERCISE: PAYING IT FORWARD (ONGOING)
Recognize the impact that others have had on you

Using the boxes below, list people who have shown you kindness and have had a positive impact on your life. This can be anyone from any phase of your life, including childhood. You can include people who are no longer alive, as well as people you have never met.

I am grateful for _____ who positively

impacted my life by _____

Each month, set a time to reflect on your journey, and add at least one name to this list.

Pick at least one person every week and write a note thanking them for the difference they made in your life. Send the note, if at all possible. Record everyone you acknowledge and why you chose them in the chart below.

Date	Grateful to	Because they	Sent note

The impact I'm having...

_____

_____

_____

_____

_____

_____

_____

_____

_____

_____

_____

_____

_____

_____

_____

_____

Questions

_____

_____

Reflections

My heart is wondering...

On my journey I will...

_____

_____

_____

_____

_____

_____

_____

_____

_____

_____

_____

_____

_____

Action

ABOUT THE ARTIST

Joanne Fink, founder of Zenspirations®, is a spiritual seeker, award-winning artist, best-selling author, and inspirational speaker. Her mission is two-fold: to help people tap into their innate creative talents and use them to make a difference in the world, and to change the culture of grief by bringing hope and healing to grieving hearts and creating tools to support the bereaved. Joanne is the author of *When You Lose Someone You Love*, *My Prayer Journal*, and the *Zenspirations®* series. To learn more about Joanne and her work, visit her websites: www.Zenspirations.com and www.WhenYouLoseSomeone.com.

ACKNOWLEDGMENTS

This book is dedicated with love and gratitude to my lifelong friend and fellow artist, Penny Tsaltas Lisk, who has been a continual source of wisdom and support throughout this journey, and my friends Tracey Lyon Nicholson, Deena Disraelly, and Dr. Susan Bach, who each read countless drafts and provided invaluable suggestions.

I am also grateful to the friends and family who provided input and encouragement, especially: Betty Abrascart, Julie Ager, Gail Beck, Lynda Cheldelin Fell, Mary Ogden Ellis, Ashley Estrela, Mary Anne Fellows, Cherish Flieder, Gladys Gonzalez, Tiffany Hill, Kathleen Hooker, Dana Kaplan, Rob Leuschke, Elizabeth Motyka, Ketra Oberlander, Kimme Prindle, Toni Popkin and Reeva Shaffer.